The Collector's Guide to
Kitchen Antiques
by Don & Carol Raycraft

Collector Books
Box 3009
Paducah, Ky 42001

Collector's Guide to Kitchen Antiques

The current values in this book should be used only as a guide. They are not intended to set prices, which vary from one section of the country to another. Auction prices as well as dealer prices vary greatly and are affected by condition as well as demand. Neither the Author nor the Publisher assumes responsibility for any losses that might be incurred as a result of consulting this guide.

Book design: Jessica Jenkins, Goodgraphiks,
            Nashville, Tn in coordination with
            Nashville Graphic Productions
Typography: Type Creations, Nashville, Tn

Printed and bound in the United States of America

Collector Books
Box 3009
Paducah, Ky 42001

—For DJR whose influence is still being felt from long ago and far away—

Acknowledgements

The following individuals contributed more than
they know to this project:

Dave & Barb Bertsche
Elmer and Marilyn Fedder
Mike and Martha Hillard
Gordon and Jean Ann Honegger
Larry and Debbie Hopkins
Capt. Alex Hood
Bill Schroeder
Bernice Veatch
Jim White

Photography
Mike Hillard
Jean Ann Honegger
Dave & Barb Bertsche
Elmer Fedder
     and
Carol Raycraft

Lighting
M.D. Raycraft
S.C. Raycraft
R.C. Raycraft
Miles Bertsche

*Don and Carol Raycraft and their
three sons, Craig, Michael, and Scott,
live in a recycled stone barn in central
Illinois.*

*They are the authors of more than a
dozen books on early Americana with
topics ranging from country pottery to
the Shakers.*

*They have been collecting early fur-
niture, baskets, pottery, textiles,
Shaker, and kitchen antiques since the
mid-1960's.*

Table of Contents

Preface

The more we are involved in collecting country antiques, the more obvious it becomes to us that to write a book of this type it is crucial that you have already paid the price of thrice cooked fast food, watered down colas, closed shops, busy signals, dead ends, barking dogs, Mexican imports from Maine, and no rooms at the inn.

Only someone who has written the lengthy letters, endured the endless and fruitless trips, and become a second son to Ma Bell by sending her outrageous checks each month can begin to put down the feelings of exhilaration that are earned by tripping over the rarest of rare at a country auction in New Hampshire on a day when everyone else stayed in bed, or in a crowded basement in Dupo, Illinois filled with golden oak, plastic curtains, Screamin' Jay Hawkins records, and an eagle butter print.

The Country Home

The fireplace was the central point of existence in the homes of Pilgrim century and colonial America. In the early days the chimneys were constructed of logs plastered with clay or marsh reeds and some type of mortar. There were obvious problems of fire with these designs and chimneys made of anything other than stone or brick were eventually outlawed. It was necessary to have regulations because a fire in one house would quickly spread to a second house and eventually the entire community would be destroyed.

Fire wardens were employed to periodically check the fireplace and chimney in each residence to guarantee safety for all the town's residents. Many towns made it mandatory that a fire ladder and heavy leather fire bucket with a bail handle be a part of the household inventory. In rural villages every adult male was a member of the fire company and was required to race to each fire at the ringing of a centrally located fire bell. Upon arriving at the fire, a well or pond were located and two lines were quickly formed. One line filled the leather buckets at the water source and passed them from hand to hand until the contents were dropped or thrown at the fire. The second line passed the empty buckets from the fire back to the well or pond to be hurriedly replenished.

After the house was destroyed or the fire put out, the fire warden was responsible for seeing that the fire buckets were returned to their owners to be rehung on a nail or peg near the fire place. Many of the leather buckets were decorated with painted scenes, initials, numbers, or family crests or names.

The fire place was the primary heat source in the simple homes of the seventeenth and early eighteenth centuries. The typical one radiated so much heat that someone sleeping six to eight feet away would be freezing only on one side of their body. Water could not be left in jugs, crocks, or bowls overnight because ice would form. Warming pans or bed warmers of copper or brass attached to a turned piece of pine or poplar were used on cold nights to provide a brief hint of warmth to a tired citizen. The pan had a hinged lid that allowed hot coals from the fire to be placed inside, carried to the bed, thrust under the covers, and moved about rapdily. The trick was to warm the bed and not to ignite the blankets and its potential occupant.

The majority of the early log houses consisted of a single room with a sleeping loft above. It was essential in such limited space that furniture be sturdy and capable of multiple uses.

In the Pilgrim century trestle tables were a common sight in frontier and country homes. The table consisted of a single board five to six feet in length and up to thirty six inches in width placed across saw horses. At the conclusion of the meal the "table board" was lifted off and leaned against the wall or under a bed. Most boards were covered while in use with a table cloth or "board cloth" of home spun material.

Among the rarest of early American tables are table boards that are a single slab of wood four to six inches thick with several "dished out" sections on the surface. These dished out areas were typically two inches deep and sixteen to eighteen inches in circumference. In homes that did not have wooden plates or trenchers, the table board served the same purpose. The indentations served as a plate that was filled with food and washed off or scrubbed down after each meal.

In a home that did have wooden plates or trenchers they were carefully cleaned and stored in a cupboard between meals. Often a single trencher would serve as a plate for two diners who alternated eating from it. Many show extensive wear on both sides as they were often turned over and used for different courses in the same meal.

The typical diner in early America made extensive use of a spoon, the knife he carried strapped to his side, his hands, and a heavy napkin that was used to clean up the damage between courses. Forks were seldom available in colonial America until the early 1700's and were still unknown in frontier America a century later.

The spoons that were used were made of wood, pewter, or from cattle horns. When pewter spoons were bent or broken beyond repair they were melted down and recast in molds that made a single spoon.

Most frontier families drank ale, beer, or wine and only occasionally water. As cows and goats began to appear in some numbers in the early 1700's, milk became more commonly available. In the Pilgrim century glass was a rare commodity that was cared for and passed on in a citizen's will to a surviving family member. At the table bottles were handed from diner to diner with little regard for sanitary precautions. Liquids were drunk from horn cups, gourds, stoneware mugs, or leather "black jacks."

Collectors who search for Pilgrim century and eighteenth century American kitchen antiques should be sure to schedule ample time for the hunt and almost unlimited funding for the trip. It is difficult to authenticate and date an early piece unless it has been handed down through a single family for two hundred and fifty years. Kitchen and hearth utensils were used daily and when cracked or chipped beyond reasonable repair they were discarded. As machine made household utensils began to be produced in the mid-1800's, the home made bowls and spoons no longer were made by local wood turners. Unlike fine pieces of silver or imported china, the woodenware of an earlier era was not carefully stored away or preserved for later generations. The pieces that have survived have done so only through oversight or accident.

There were no Big Macs or Pepe Tacos in New England in 1800 but there were daily meals that we can only stand in awe of today. An individual with a weakness for sea food or wild game could plan evening menus around venison, wild turkey, pigeon, squirrel, rabbit, pheasant, partridge, duck, sturgeon, oysters, salmon, shad, lobster, quail, and curlew. Vegetables included squash, peas, parsnips, carrots, turnips, and stewed pumpkin. Potatoes were available but not commonly eaten in New England due to persistent rumors that they, like bathing, were potentially dangerous to the health.

Taking the place of potatoes as a daily staple were hasty pudding, corn or apple dumplings, and corn meal porridge. The pudding was slowly produced and hastily eaten from a mixture of oatmeal or wheat flour and milk.

A touch of sweetness was provided through maple syrup and maple sugar, honey, or sugar cut from cones that weighed up to ten pounds.

Figure 1 Dry sink-bucket bench, pine, C. 1850

This kitchen piece was used for the serving and preparation of food. It was also used for a variety of kitchen related chores. The work surface is criss-crossed with cuts and scratches from a chopping knife and discolored from food stains, liquids, and daily scrubbings. The single, dovetailed drawer was for storing knives, forks, and other cooking and cleaning utensils.

The curd or cheese basket was found in western New York and dates from nineteenth century. Its diameter of 27" is exceptional for a hexagon woven basket of oak splint.

Figure 1

Figure 2

Figure 3 Dry sink, pine, early form, found in New York, c. 1840

Figure 2 Dry sink, red paint, unusual extended trough, mid-nineteenth century

One of the first pieces of furniture that collectors of country antiques searched for in the early 1960's was a dry sink. They turned up with much greater regularity in the midwest, Ohio, and Pennsylvania than in New England. Today even simple sinks with a trough, two doors below, and several coats of paint are uncommon.

The dry sink began its life as a simple bench for buckets, evolved into a more elaborate bench with several shelves, and eventually emerged with doors covering the bottom shelf and a trough and splash board to keep water from decorating the wall.

The sinks were popular in middle America from the mid-nineteenth century until the coming of indoor plumbing during the first quarter of the twentieth century. The typical sink had a trough lined with zinc and was made from pine. The hardware was almost always factory made and consisted of butt hinges and spring catches with porcelain knobs to keep the doors closed.

Sinks with a drawer for tableware, a high back and three overhead drawers, or constructed of walnut or cherry are less commonly found.

Figure 4

Figure 5

Figure 4 Chimney cupboard, pine, painted blue, found in New York, c. 1830-1840

This cupboard was built into a rectangular opening in a fireplace with a wall of bricks separating it from the fire. It was designed to keep food warm while the rest of the meal was being prepared or the husband was too long in the fields. Most chimney cupboards are "blind fronts" and measure 30" to 36" wide and 5'6" to 6' tall. A cupboard that was originally built into a house, as was this example, is referred to as an architectural cupboard.

Figure 5 Pine bucket bench, Pennsylvania, early nineteenth century

This bench had been grained with mustard paint to resemble oak when we found it. The heavy use and little regard that bucket benches faced each day had worn much of the later paint down to a point where the original red peaked through.

Bucket benches are found in a variety of forms ranging from simple, low benches that graced the back porch and front yard on wash day to more elaborately constructed examples.

The benches were used for storing buckets, brushes, soaps, and other wash day equipment.

Figure 6 Bucket bench, found in southwestern Ohio, c. 1850-1860

Figure 7 Desk-box, New England, hinged lift top, pine, mid-nineteenth century.

With the addition of legs this desk becomes a desk-on-frame or a school master's desk. The interior of this desk-box has several pigeonholes for storing papers. These desks were used in nineteenth century homes for keeping household and business papers.

Figure 8 Small kitchen storage cupboard, Ohio, nineteenth century

Figure 9 Apothecary chest, New England, pine, c. 1840

Figure 10 Apothecary chest, New England, pine, c. 1840

This thirty-five drawer apothecary chest was originally built into a wall of shelves in a New England country store. The stenciled names of the drawers include senna, coloured balls, mustard, black lead, thread, maple sugar and black silk. Note the lighter colored pine board on the end of the chest in Figure 9. This board was added to the chest at the point it was built into the wall of the store. There are no saw marks on the ends of the chest which would indicate it had been cut from a longer section.

Figure 11 Apothecary chest, found in Massachusetts, c. 1830-1850

Figure 12 Pine cradle, New England, c. 1830-1850

The pine cradle has two pegs protruding from each side that allowed a rope to be securely tied across the top of the cradle. This provided a frontier infant's mother with the illusion of security while she dozed in a nearby bed. The cradle appears to be in "original" paint. This suggests that it has not been repainted, refinished, or refreshed in anyway. If it was in "early paint" it would be in similar condition but repainted one or more times.
In the background is a rare Shaker tilter chair from Mt. Lebanon, New York.

Figure 13 Hooded cradle, New England, c. 1830-1850

Figure 14 Step-back cupboard, pine, c. 1860. ▶

A cupboard with a "glazed" front has "lights" or individual panes of glass. This cupboard or "dish dresser" also has two drawers for storage and a larger area with two doors and shelves below. The upper case or top of the cupboard is recessed or "stepped back" from the lower case or bottom.

Figure 15 Child's dish dresser or cupboard, c. 1880.

This miniature cupboard measures 30" x 16" and was found in southwestern Illinois. It is from the collection of Sarah Fedder of Winchester, Illinois.

Figure 14

Figure 16 Pine, "blind front" cupboard, mid-nineteenth century.

A cupboard that is not "glazed" is referred to as a "blind front". The red paint is "early" but not the "original" paint. A man who works for a natural gas company called several years ago and indicated he had a cupboard he wanted to sell. He had found it in a local basement while reading a meter and purchased it from an elderly lady whose family had brought it to Illinois from Ohio in the late nineteenth century.

When a collector buys a piece of early furniture seldom does he receive an accurate history or "provenance" of the piece. The furniture has passed through so many retail and wholesale hands that any record of ownership is quickly lost.

Figure 17 & 18 Step-back cupboard, New England, mid-nineteenth century

Figure 19 Chair table, pine, New England, c. 1830
This scrubbed top table has a diameter of only 35''. It was used in an early home where space was at a premium and a piece of furniture often was forced to serve multiple uses.

Figure 20

Figure 21

Figure 22 Apple sorter's chair, splint seat, New England, mid-nineteenth century

This chair was designed for a sorter to relax while picking the "goods" from the "bads" and the reds from the yellows.

Figure 20 Shaker rocking chairs, Mt. Lebanon, N.Y., late nineteenth century

A common sight in front of the fire places of most nineteenth century homes was a rocking chair. Ben Franklin is given credit by several historians for adding rockers from a broken cradle to a straight chair and developing the rocking chair in the mid-1700's.

The Shakers sold rocking chairs in eight sizes (0-7) from their Mt. Lebanon, New York community well into the twentieth century. These two examples are impressed with the number "7" (the largest size) on the back of the top slat of each chair.

The bar or rail attached to the top of the chair was used to tie a cushion.

Figure 21 Rocking settee or "mammy" bench, c. 1840

A mammy's bench was another form of the rocking chair found near the fire place. The removeable gate allowed the child to sleep comfortably without the risk of rolling onto the floor while the mother rocked.

This bench is a rod-back with arms of cherry and a pine seat. The crest rail of the bench was heavily stenciled to add a touch of color.

Figure 23 Child's slat-back or ladder-back arm chair, taped seat, Ohio, c. 1850

The taped seat in this early child's chair was a late replacement. The original seat was made of oak or ash splint. Carefully studying a chair or piece of furniture can provide some interesting insights. The paint on the front arm supports and legs has been completely worn down and the surface is now flat rather than round.

The chair was used as a walker by a nameless child who tipped it over, held it firmly by the back legs and pushed it across many miles of wooden floors while he learned to negotiate on his own.

Figure 24 Slat-back or ladder-back side chair, original paint, splint seat, c. 1840-1860

Collectors should carefully study the obvious points of wear on early side chairs. The back of the finials or turnings on the rear posts should be almost flat from being forcefully leaned against the wall. The two front stretchers or rungs on this chair show heavy use from hundreds of heels being braced or hooked over and under the stretchers for many years.

Figure 25 Country slat-back or ladder-back kitchen chair, early paint, handcrafted, replaced splint seat, New England, first half of the nineteenth century.

Figure 26

Figure 27

Figure 26 Half-spindle, thumb-back kitchen chair, factory made, possibly Pennsylvania, mid-nineteenth century.

Kitchen chairs of this type were sold in sets of six or eight from the 1840's through the 1870's. The chairs were painted with a background coat of dark green, brown, yellow, red, or black and then stenciled. The crest rail or top slat was stenciled with fruits, flowers, or birds and the plank seat of pine was outlined with a brush as were the spindles and stretchers.

It is unusual to find a set of six chairs that have survived without being lost, broken, or repainted. A collector who finds four chairs with much of the original paint and stenciling is fortunate today.

Figure 27 Arrow-back, plank bottom, kitchen chair, possibly Pennsylvania, mid-nineteenth century.

The stenciled decoration on the crest rail has been worn down to the base coat of red paint.

Lighting

The earliest American homes were lit after the sun went down by fire light or "candle wood" Pine knots or slices of pitch pine were burned to generate a meager light source in the simple New England homes. The pine was cut to candle size and burned like a torch that generated light, a great deal of smoke, and a tar like substance that freely fell to the floor. Various kinds of tripod based or spike driven iron "cressets" were designed to hold the flaming wood.

Another solid fuel lighting device was the split or rush light. The rush light with counter weighted jaws and an occasional socket for a tallow candle were in use in America for well over two hundred years. A supply of rushes from nearby streams or marsh lands was available to most homeowners in New England. The pith was removed from rush, dipped in grease or tallow and allowed to harden. Various kinds of grasses were treated in the same manner and used in the iron lamps when rushes were not readily available.

There is a major problem for collectors of early lighting in general and rush lights or grease lamps in particular. It is almost impossible to differentiate the country of origin for many of the individual pieces of lighting. The same forms were more commonly found in England, Ireland, and Wales than in New England. It is equally as difficult to accurately date the lamps as to assign a country or specific area as the origin. Man has been burning fluids and animal fat as a light source for thousands of years.

The earliest rush lights did not have candle sockets because beef tallow for the production of candles was not available in even limited quantities until the late 1600's.

It was a major problem to find substitutes for tallow and eventually wax from honeycombs and spermaceti were found to be adequate. Spermaceti is a waxy substance obtained from the head of the sperm whale in a thick, oily form. Twelve to fifteen pounds of spermaceti could be found in a single sperm whale.

In the mid-1600's it was possible to hunt for whales along the eastern seaboard in small boats. As the decade wore on the boats were forced to gradually lengthen their journeys and the size of their ships until by 1780, the whale hunters were gone for months. Spermaceti became very expensive and it was necessary to search for other materials for candles. Spermaceti was popular because it generated several times the flame and light of tallow candles.

An additional source of wax for candles was the bayberry or candleberry that grew in clusters on the stem of the bayberry shrub (Myrica pensylvanica) which grows along the Atlantic coast. The berries were carefully picked, slowly boiled, and repeatedly skimmed until the wax took on a light green color. A bushel of berries produces only four or five pounds of wax. The bayberry candle was resistent to melting in storage, burned more slowly, produced little smoke, and emitted a light and pleasant odor after being extinguished.

Several Massachusetts communities passed laws in the 1680's prohibiting or limiting the picking of bayberries. One town made the picking of berries prior to September 15 subject to a heavy fine.

Producing Candles

Candles were produced at home by a dipping process that allowed wax to gradually build upon a wick or through the use of candlemolds. The months of October and early November were the primary months for butchering and building up stores of food for the winter. The fat that was left over after the butchering of cattle was placed in an iron kettle over the fire. The kettle was filled with water. The tallow was reheated and skimmed repeatedly until it appeared to be almost pure. Two poles were placed across the top slats of two chairs that were usually four to six feet apart. A series of sticks like rungs in a ladder were put across the 18" to 24" gap between the two poles. Each stick had four to six cotton or spun hemp wicks tied to it. In an orderly fashion each stick with its knotted wicks was dipped into the kettle of simmering tallow. The process was a lengthy one with the tallow gradually building up with each trip down the rungs or rows of sticks. The primary trick was to keep the tallow at such a temperature that each successive dipping would not melt the tallow already on the wick. If the tallow was too cool it would develop lumps and bumps that limited the candle's ability to burn evenly.

Figure 28 Slide top candlebox, chipped carved, New England, eighteenth century, carved from single block of wood, 17" x 3½" x 3" high

Candlemolds may be found that are made from tin, red-ware, or pewter. The redware and pewter molds are found in a pine frame that contains twenty to thirty six individual barrels or tubes. The vast majority of the surviving candlemolds were made of tin and range in size from four to twelve tubes. Molds that made an odd number of candles (3, 5, 7, 9) are uncommon as are larger molds that included 24, 36, 48 or 96 tubes.

The wicks used in making candles were normally made from cotton. Four to eight strands of the spun material were twisted together into a single wick. A major problem was keeping the wicks taut within the tubes of the candlemold. The wicks were threaded through the bottom of the mold and knotted. The top of the wick was tied to a wire or stick that ran the length of the row of ''holes''. After the tallow was poured into the molds it took from fifteen to forty five minutes to harden at room temperature. The knots at the base of the mold were cut and the entire row of 3, 4, or 6 candles could be lifted out of the mold by picking up the wick sticks or wires. When the candles could not be easily lifted from the mold a hot water bath was prepared and the mold was plunged in and out. This normally loosened any tallow sticking to the sides of the tubes and the candles emerged from the mold with little trouble. The large molds that made as many as twelve dozen candles at a time were used by chandlers or professional candlemakers who traveled from village to village in the early 1800's trading their skill and gossip from the other side of the county for food and lodging.

Molded and dipped candles were stored in wooden or tin candle boxes to keep them from yellowing due to ex-posure to the air. The wooden boxes were normally made of soft wood (pine or poplar) with a sliding cover that was beveled or chamfered on its sides. Some boxes were designed to be hung from the wall and others were used on the table.

In many early houses a small table or stand near the stairs contained several saucer based candleholders with ring handles and a filled candle box. The candlesticks and lighted candles were used to negotiate the stairs on dark evenings. In some houses a niche or small opening was constructed in the wall at the base of the stairs for the candlesticks and candle box.

Figure 29

Figure 30

Figure 29 Painted leather fire bucket, Massachusetts, c. 1840

This leather fire bucket is in excellent repair and is alledged to have come from Martha's Vineyard. It is also possible its original owner may have been Martin Vance or Mary Murphy. Elaborately decorated fire buckets with action scenes or family crests command many hundreds of dollars when offered at an auction block or in an antique shop.

If a fire bucket has been repainted or had a handle replaced its value would be dramatically reduced.

Cloth fire bags were kept in the leather buckets for filling with family treasures in case of fire. On December 9, 1979 a fire bag marked ''N. Marsh'' sold for $90 at a Concord, New Hampshire auction.

Figure 30 Combination rush holder, early nineteenth century

This particular rush light also has a socket for a candle. It is very difficult to determine if a rush light was made in America or the British Isles. When this light was purchased, it was indicated that it was American but that was second or fourth hand information passed on from seller to buyer.

Matches

One of the great rarities for collectors to trip over is an artifact from the daily life of a resident of the early 1800's. Simple items such as matches, food containers, and clothing are probably the most difficult to find. The china, silver, and imported furniture that were passed from one generation to another survive in far greater quantities than a farmer's shoes, his wife's cooking utensils, or the bed they shared.

When new inventions or improved processes filtered down to the frontier cabins or small villages, life slowly became easier. The difficulties in providing artificial lighting in early homes were slowly resolved by the use of candlewood, burning fluid lamps, tallow or wax candles, whale oil and eventually, kerosene. Each step was a major improvement in the manner in which people were able to conduct their daily lives. The problems of odors, smoke, and enough light grew less with each improved lighting source.

A major change in people's life styles occured in the late 1820's with the development of phosphorus matches. Matches were sold in small boxes of one hundred with a piece of sand paper to ignite it. A serious difficulty was finding a wood that burned slowly enough to provide adequate light.

Prior to the advent of friction matches householders were forced to utilize hot coals or tinder boxes to start fires. A tinder box was a small tin box filled with scraps of paper and linen cloth (tinder) that would catch fire from the sparks given off by striking a piece of flint against a piece of iron.

Figure 31

Figure 32

Figure 31 Iron trammel candle holder, American, c. 1800

Trammels have been commonly found in household inventories and kitchens since the Middle Ages. They were made from iron and were used within the fireplace to adjust the height of simmering soups, meat, or stew above the burning fire at precisely the distance selected by the cook.

Trammel lighting devices allowed a reader to adjust the sawtooth ratchet to a height that met the lighting needs of an individual reading the family Bible or repairing a damaged sock.

The quality of workmanship in this lighting device strongly suggests that it was made in New England rather than Europe.

Figure 32 Candle dip, New England, early nineteenth century, painted red

The candle dip allowed a dozen wicks to be tied to the wire hooks and periodically be lowered into the kettle of simmering wax or tallow. This example was probably part of a revolving stand with eight to ten arms that had a candle dip hanging from each arm.

Figure 32A Rare 12 tube circular candle mold, probably Ohio, mid-nineteenth century.

A copy of the *Magazine Antiques* from 1928 describes an Ohio tinsmith who found himself with an excessive number of tin pie plates that he could not sell. After much deliberation he decided to use the pie plates in the construction of circular candlemolds which he could then sell more easily. When a collector finds an unusual piece of furniture, lighting, or wooden-ware and attempts to understand why it was constructed as it was, he seldom knows if his speculations are correct. We feel that one of the Ohio tinsmith's candlemolds has endured for over a century and entered our collection with an explanation for its uncommon form.

We purchased the circular mold in 1966 for $225 from a midwestern dealer. At that point in time $225 was a whole lot of money to pay for a candlemold when dry sinks could be found for $90 and bird-decorated stoneware crocks and jugs were commonly sold for $50. The decision to purchase it was a hasty one and my wife almost expired from dehydration after crying for one hundred and fifty miles on the way home.

Figure 33 Miniature tin candlemold, 5½" high, c. 1880

The miniature twelve tube mold with a strap handle was used in making candles for Christmas trees in an era before electricity reached most homes. At that time it was easier to burn down your house with Christmas lights than it is today, even with the advantages of frayed and over loaded extension cords.

Figure 34 Footed tin candle mold, 13" tall, c. 1860

We began a candlemold collection in the mid-1960's when common molds were general-ly sold for about $2 to $3 a tube. The obvious exceptions to this were the odd numbered molds (3, 5, 7, 9, 13) or molds with an uncommon form. The footed candlemold was pur-chased for about $65. It is the only mold of its form that we have ever had the opportunity to purchase.

Figure 35 Twelve tube copper mold, c. 1860

Candlemolds in a frame or battery are normally made of tin, pewter, or redware pottery. Hanging or standing molds are almost always made of tin. This twelve tube mold with two strap handles is made of copper.

Figure 32A

Figure 33

Figure 34

Figure 35

Figure 36 Two tube candlemold, tin, found in Massachusetts, c. 1850

Figure 37 Twelve and twenty four tube tin candlemolds, iron "hogscraper" candle stick, mid-nineteenth century.

Figure 38 Blue painted candle box, pine, New York, c. 1840.

It was essential that tallow candles be kept out of the sunlight after being dipped or molded. There are many variations of candle boxes that were used as containers. Hanging boxes of wood or tin and examples similar to this one that were designed for setting on a table may be found. Early candle boxes are usually painted red, mustard, or blue. If the box has not been repainted or refinished its value will usually be enhanced.

Figure 39 Tin candle box, painted black, New England, c. 1860

Tin candle containers were crafted and sold by traveling tinsmiths from the early 1800's until the rise of factory-made goods in the late 1860's. This example is from the factory period and is in excellent original condition.

In recent years there has been a wealth of reproductions and fake tin candle boxes made from scraps of a hundred tin roofs or artificially aged with acid. A collector of tin kitchen or hearth implements should carefully inspect the edges of the tin and search for marks of wear. If the piece has been recently cut with tin snips the edges would have a shiney surface with no wear or patina.

On the beam above the candle box are some Shaker made wick sticks bound with a piece of home spun. These sticks were used to catch a flame from the fire and light candles or whale oil lanterns. They were found in an attic in New Hampshire.

Figure 40 Tin petticoat lamp, kerosene, c. 1860

Kerosene became a major fuel to provide a clean, efficient, and relatively inexpensive light source in the early 1860's and continued for almost eighty years to be utilized in American homes. Electric lights became a luxury in eastern cities in 1900. Many areas of the rural midwest did not receive electricity until the late 1930's.

Figure 41 Wall lamp, tin, kerosene, c. late nineteenth century

Figure 42 Miniature lamp, kerosene, used as a night light, c. early 1900's.

Woodenware

The first settlers who left the relative comforts of New England in the early 1800's and traveled to Ohio, Indiana, and Kentucky literally lived in an age of wood. From the hinges and locks on the door to the tools and kitchen implements that were in use each day from sun up to the shadows of evening, these people relied on a wide assortment of carefully selected woods to meet their needs.

Each small community had a joiner and a cooper who traded their skills for a meager living. Joiners produced chairs, beds, tables, and cupboards and coopers made barrels, kegs, buckets, tubs, keelers, and churns.

Each piece of wood the joiner utilized in the construction of a chair was purposefully chosen to meet a specific need. Maple was a common choice for the legs and pine was often used in the making of the seat. The stretchers and arm supports were oak, maple, beech, or hickory. The bow or curved back of many chairs was initially steamed to make it pliable and then shaped from ash, hickory, or oak. The spindles were normally either hickory or maple depending on how much flexibility was needed in the back of the chair.

The cooper also chose woods that would meet his specific needs in constructing a staved butter churn or a nest of pantry boxes.

In making a pantry box the sides and rims were made of steamed maple and the top and bottom of pine. Tiny pegs of birch were used to hold the box together along with copper or iron tacks. White pine was generally selected for staves in churns or buckets. The pine was not affected by prolonged contact with liquids, left no added taste or odor to its contents, and was plentiful and easy to work with in the shop. To tightly bind the staved churns and make them water tight, birch or hickory were chosen.

The single most popular tree in the forest for making bowls, rolling pins, clothes pins, butter molds and prints, spoons, and plates was maple. The maple is a slow growing hardwood with a tight grain that holds up well under heavy use. It maintains a smooth surface and does not splinter even after prolonged exposure to water. The vast majority of hand crafted and factory produced wooden kitchen implements that survive today are made of maple.

The life of the country cooper was altered forever in the years immediately following the Civil War. From 1860 to 1864 there was a massive war time effort to establish a variety of industries that could arm, outfit, and equip an army. With the war drawing to an inevitable end the industrialists saw that their investments must be used to find new markets. The face of America had changed during the war years because thousands of people had left rural areas to move to the growing cities for jobs in the factories. It was determined that the factories turn from producing uniforms to suits and dresses and from bullets to butter, buttons, and brooms. For the first time mass produced

Figure 43 Apple butter bucket, bail handle, 11" tall, grey paint and paper label, c. 1880.

household goods were now available throughout the nation. In the 1870's and 1880's several mail order houses in Chicago and New York opened their doors, the wallets of consumers, and started a new form of marketing goods.

The cooper and joiner soon faced levels of competition that forced most of them out of business and ended a period in American history when craftsmenship was king and utility and simplicity were in style. What followed was an age of veneered knick knack shelves filled with massed produced taste and salt and pepper shakers to meet every need.

It has been down the long hill ever since.

Treenware

The word "treen" or "treene" has been a part of the English language since the 13th century. In general, treen refers to the day-to-day wooden pieces that were used in eating or preparing food to be eaten. These functional items of wood include spoons, bowls, plates, mortars and pestles, simple food molds, and countless other small wooden household tools.

Collecting Woodenware

As we have repeatedly written, most woodenware or treenware in the eighteenth and nineteenth centuries was made to be strictly utilitarian in function. The spoons, bowls, and various molds were designed to be used and relatively few have survived intact. There was no reason to store old kitchen implements when the factory age brought massed produced goods into the house. Many of the early pieces of woodenware that have

Figure 44 Mortar and pestle, maple, mid-nineteenth century.

Figure 45 Butter print or stamp, New England, 4¼" diameter, hand carved, c. 1840-1850

Figure 46 Butter print, uncommon form, Hudson River Valley of New York, maple, late eighteenth-early nineteenth century, 4½" wide x 9¼" long.

Figure 47 Butter molds, one-half pound and one pound, machine impressed decoration, maple, late nineteenth century.

Figure 48 Butter molds, maple, late nineteenth century.

survived have been stripped of their patina of use and abuse, coated with an artificial glimmer, and hung on the plastic barn siding walls of contemporary split levels.

To find American made, hand crafted kitchen tools in their original form is almost a feat of legerdemain. The problem is greatly complicated by the importation of a wide variety of kitchen and hearth "antiques" in wood, iron, and tin from Portugal, Spain, Yugoslavia, and Mexico that began in quantity in the mid-1960's. Many of these items were still being used in homes on the day of their purchase. A hand crafted maple spoon in constant use for a decade appears to a collector to have come over on the Mayflower. Several of the importers publish catalogs of their offerings. Collectors will be amazed after studying the catalogs to see the large number of imports that appear in shows, at shops, and often in their own collections.

There are many collectors who limit their hunt to wooden sugar, butter, gingerbread, and cookie molds and prints. The difficulty in determining the country of origin is especially prevalent in the area of wooden molds. Wood carvers in Holland and Belgium have been making molds for bakeries for several hundred years. They probably made a few yesterday too.

Architects in Europe have commissioned the same wood carvers to make boards for them with the carved images of animals, angels, and geometric designs. Plaster is poured into the molds and allowed to form. The finished product is used to add a decorator's touch to mirrors, picture frames, ceilings, and walls. These boards usually have a second board nailed or screwed to them as backing. The "cookie" or gingerbread molds normally do not have the second board. It is not uncommon to find "plaster" molds with or without the backing board being sold as "cookie" molds. If the gingerbread or "cookie" molds show evidence of being burned a second problem exists. The food molds never came into contact with the oven intentionally. They were a molding tool that only provided a shape for the pastry or sugar candy to take. In recent years many molds, that in reality are younger than the collector who purchases them, have been artificially aged with worm holes from a drill bit and fire marks to show heavy use. The majority of the old and new European molds are made of boxwood.

Identifying and Dating Woodenware

In attempting to identify the particular wood from which a given piece is made, many problems are encountered in an accurate investigation. The scientific procedure is to make a microscopic study of a carefully sliced portion of the end grain of the wood. A three dimensional piece about the size of a pencil eraser is ideal for most investigations. A skilled wood analyst can normally determine the specific variety of tree from which the piece was made. He can also indicate whether that tree was native to North America, Europe, or wherever. Most people obviously do not utilize the services of wood analysis on many occasions during their collecting careers. They attempt by studying the color, weight, and grain of the wood to make their own determination.

Figure 49   Wooden wash bowl, chestnut, diameter of 11" x 6" high, New England, c. early 1800's.

This is not a simple proposition because the exposure to grease, food, wine, and water over a lengthy period of time dramatically alters the color of wood and changes its appearance. The color is also altered by age and exposure to light.

There is a staggering statistic that reports there have been a minimum of 50,000 varieties of hard wood and more than 100 varieties of softwood specifically identified world wide.

Many times it is equally difficult to date a piece of woodenware as it is to determine from what tree it was made. Wooden plates, bowls, spoons, and kitchen implements seldom carry any type of maker's mark that aids in the dating process. Unlike a piece of Bennington stoneware that carries an impressed signature in its neck that limits the time it could have been made to within a decade or two, woodenware almost never provides the collector with such clues. The difficulty is compounded by the fact that the processes involved in producing hand crafted woodenware changed little from the Pilgrim century until the mid-1800's.

Figure 50 Chopping knife, factory made, maple handle, c. 1880-1900.

Figure 51 Shaker, staved berry bucket, bail handle, yellow paint, New England, late nineteenth century.

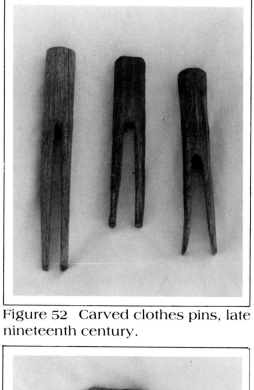

Figure 52 Carved clothes pins, late nineteenth century.

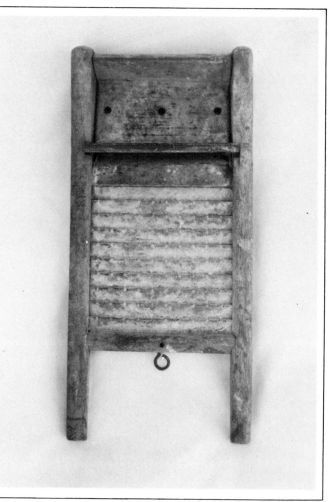

Figure 53 Wash or scrubbing board, c. 1850.

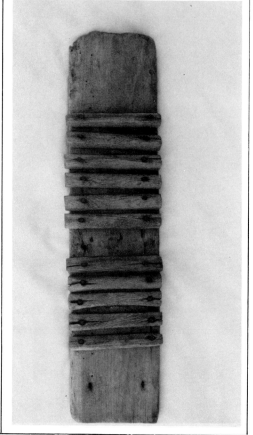

Figure 54 Scrubbing stick, 24" long, c. 1830.

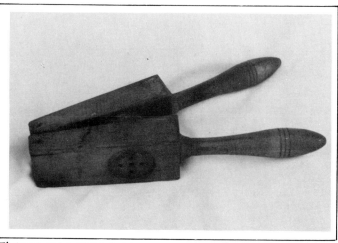

Figure 55 Lemon squeezer, maple, early factory period, c. 1850-1875

Figure 56 Butterprint and buttermolds, maple, nineteenth century.

The value of a print or mold is largely determined by the decoration it carries. Birds and animals are rare and flowers, leaves, shocks of wheat, and geometric patterns are more commonly found. On early prints or molds the designs were hand carved on the maple surface. After 1860 most of the designs were machine stamped into the heavily steamed and pliable wood.

It is extremely difficult to determine if the print or mold was made in the United States or imported from Europe. Similar forms and designs were used in England, Scandinavia, Germany, and the United States.

Figure 57 Eagle butter print, mold with leaf design, and rectangular double "wheat" stamp, nineteenth century.

The typical factory made mold was made of maple and consisted of three pieces. These included the cup or bell, the round print with a design impressed into it, and a plunger or handle. The handle was threaded to fit into the back of the print.

Figure 58 Dasher butter churn, button-hole hoops, Shaker made, piggin handle, New England, first half of the nineteenth century.

Figure 60 Rocking butter churn, pine, found in Lancaster County, Pennsylvania, c. 1850.

Figure 59 Tin butter churn, maple dasher, New England, Shaker made, nineteenth century.

Figure 61 Burl bowl and burl butter worker, American, early nineteenth century.

The grain in a slice of "knot wood" or burl is randomly spaced. There is no ordinary growth pattern or obvious grain as there is in other woods. Cracks or breaks in wood normally occur along or "with" the grain. As burl has no precise pattern of graining, it seldom splits or cracks even after hard use.

Colonists in the Pilgrim century learned the advantages of using burl from the Indians. The colonists turned their bowls on spring pole lathes and used chisels and wooden mallets to finish the bowls.

Figure 62 Maple storage or work bowl, New England, early nineteenth century, 27½'' x 8½'' x 6'' high.

Figure 63 Maple bowls, factory-made, painted, ranging in diameter from 5'' to 10'', late nineteenth century.

Though thousands of maple bowls in a multitude of sizes were turned out by woodenware factories in the late 1800's, only a relatively few survive intact. Like all kitchen utensils, these bowls were produced to be in daily use. They were used for serving, mixing, and chopping various foods. After being exposed to hundreds of scrubbings and poundings most were retired to the fireplace to provide a good start to a long night's fire.

Figure 64 Maple bowl, 14'' diameter, late nineteenth century.

Figure 65 Maple bowl, 12½" diameter, late nineteenth century.

Figure 66

Figure 66
Meat ladder, Pennsylvania,
c. mid-nineteenth century
Copper apple butter kettle,
southern Illinois, c. 1880-1900.

Figure 67

Meat ladders were hung by both ends from ceiling beams in front of the hearth. Dried meats were tied by their wrapping strings and allowed to hang down. Individual pieces or sections of meat could be cut and eaten or used in cooking over the open fire.

Apple butter kettles with iron bail handles were a common sight at closing out farm sales and estate auctions in apple growing regions of southern Illinois in the late 1950's and early 1960's. This particular example was purchased covered with many seasons' accumulation of carbon.

Figure 67 Pine dough or bread tray, found in Vermont, c. 1840

A dough tray was used for mixing dough for bread and for allowing the dough to rise.

Figure 68 Lathe-turned, clamp-on pin cushion, maple, homespun cushion cover, New England, c. 1830.

Figure 69 Shaker cheese boxes, eyelet or button hoops,14" to 18" in diameter, New England, nineteenth century.

Figure 70 Document or storage box, pine with mahogany graining, commercially made lock, found in western Massachusetts, c. 1850-1860, 8" deep, 12" long, 5" high.

Figure 71 Flat broom, birch splint, bound with iron, turned maple handle, c. 1850.

Figure 72 Staved butter tub, Shaker fingered measure and woven horse hair sieve, New England, nineteenth century.

Figure 73 Sugar bucket, button hole or eyelet hoops, bail handle, found in Vermont, c. 1850-1870.

Figure 74 Shaker keeler, pine, staved construction, New England, mid-nineteenth century

A keeler was used to hold milk while it was cooling. This oval keeler is bound with buttonhole hoops and is painted gray.

Figure 75 Stack of seven painted firkins or sugar buckets.

Figure 76 Painted boxes with bail handles, 14'' diameter and 11'' diameter, New England, late nineteenth century.

Figure 77 Canteen, Shaker, New England, buttonhole or eyelet hoops, first half of the nineteenth century.

Figure 78 Woven horse hair sieve, Shaker, 9½'' diameter, c. 1880-1900

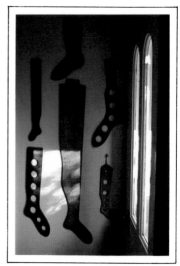

Figure 79 Sock stretchers, factory made, maple, c. 1880-1910

The large sock stretcher could have belonged to the Abominable Snow Man's mother for use on his woolen socks.

Fig. 80 Slaw cutter and spice box, factory-made, early twentieth century.

Once a spice box has been refinished it is extremely difficult to determine its age. The boxes were machine cut and then assembled by hand. They were a part of every kitchen in 1900 and were produced in a variety of forms. The majority had the name of the spice or seasoning impressed into the drawer front and had porcelain or wooden knobs. The drawers were tacked together with round headed nails and the back of the box was typically a single piece of thin pine or poplar.

Figure 81 Rolling pins, stoneware and maple, c. 1880-1910.

The majority of rolling pins that are still being discovered by collectors are factory-made of maple. The stoneware pins with advertising were often premiums for purchasing a certain quantity of groceries, customer Christmas gifts, or handed out at grand openings of new stores. The grooved maple rolling pin was used in preparing cookie dough for the oven.

Figure 82

Figure 83

Figure 82 Chopping bowl, rolling pins and butter molds, late nineteenth century
Compare the two forms that butter molds produced after 1860 may take. The rectangular "box" mold contains machine cut dovetails at its corners and carries a simple decoration impressed into its stamp.

Figure 83 Piggin, possibly European, replaced iron band, c. late nineteenth-early twentieth century.
A piggin is similar to a bucket with the distinctive characteristic of a single extended handle. Piggins were used as dippers and also for carrying feed to barnyard animals.

Figure 84 Maple sugar mold and cookie or pastry print, New England, c. 1850-1875

Figure 85

Figure 86

Figure 85 Stack of eleven Shaker boxes, New England, nineteenth century

The Shakers used fingers or "lappers" to regulate the expansion and contraction of the box.

Figure 86 Four oval Shaker boxes.

Figure 87 Large Shaker, oval, fingered box, New England, early nineteenth century, 18'' x 12'' x 5½'' high.

Figure 88 Shaker, fingered carriers, New England, late nineteenth century

Figure 89 Factory made pantry boxes, late nineteenth-early twentieth century

Figure 90 Serving tray, New England, c. 1860
Painted pantry and pill boxes, late nineteenth century Shaker berry bucket, New England, late nineteenth century. Shaker made clothes brush, New England, c. 1900. Shaker made open tub, New England, nineteenth century.

Pottery

The first potters in the American colonies began turning out redware jugs, crocks, and milk pans in the 1640's. From the Pilgrim century until the first quarter of the twentieth century redware and stoneware were an essential part of the American kitchen. In the years prior to even rudimentary refrigeration crocks, jugs, and jars were excellent for storage of food, plentiful, inexpensive, and easily cleaned.

The first stoneware in any quantity began to be produced in the 1720's. Very little stoneware from the eighteenth century has survived intact. It was produced to be utilized on a daily basis. When a piece was severely chipped, cracked, or no longer water tight, it was thrown away.

The early potters who impressed their marks into the necks of their jugs included Thomas Commeraw, Clarkson Crolius, and John Remmey. All three potters worked in New York City before 1800. A piece of stoneware carrying the mark of any of the three would be worth many hundreds of dollars today.

There was a tendency for several generations in a family to carry on the craft. Crolius's work was maintained by his son, Clarkson Crolius Jr. until the mid-nineteenth century. The pottery of John Norton was opened in 1793 in Bennington, Vermont and managed by the Norton family and various partners until 1894.

During the century of its existence the pottery used twenty nine different marks on its wares. These different marks provide the collector with an opportunity to secure a relative date for a particular piece. For example, a jug with an "E and LP Norton/ Bennington, Vermont" mark was made at some point within the 1861-1881 time frame.

A piece marked "E. Norton Bennington Vt:" could only have been made between 1859 and 1861. This opportunity to date stoneware by its mark is not limited to the pieces produced in Bennington. Almost all potteries impressed their marks into some of their works. Below is an abbreviated listing of several potteries and their estimated dates of operation. The potteries opened and closed their doors with such regularity that dating is always a series of educated guesses.

A.K. Ballard, Burlington, Vt. (1856-72) C.W. Braun, Buffalo, New York (1855-65) Cowden and Wilcox, Harrisburg, Pa. (1868-90) Fort Edward Pottery Co., Fort Edward, N.Y. (1870-85) Fort Edward Stoneware Co., Fort Edward, N.Y. (1860-90) Geddes Stoneware Pottery Co., Geddes, N.Y. (1875-1890) Hamilton and Jones, Greensboro, Pa. (1868-1880) Charles Hart, Sherburne, N.Y. (1840-80) Ottman Bros., Fort Edward, N.Y. (1860-80) Peoria Pottery Co., Peoria, Il. (1870-1900) Satterlee and Morey, Fort Edward, N.Y. (1860-95) West Troy Pottery, West Troy, N.Y. (1870-80) White (Noah, N., Noah Jr.) Binghampton and Utica, N.Y. (1828-90)

We have selected these marks because we have purchased an example from each of the cited potteries in the past year. This indicates that they are still available to collectors who will spend the time and endure the trouble to search.

Stoneware jugs may also be dated by the relative shape of the jug. A jug from Bennington that was made in 1830 would appear to be almost pear shaped or ovoid in form. The shoulders of the jug are much wider than the base. As the nineteenth century wore on the stoneware changed form dramatically. After 1850 jugs took on a gradually increasing cylindrical form until by 1880 the sides were perpendicular.

The products of the potteries were sold within a limited geographic region around the pottery. Transportation was a major problem and broken pieces commanded a very small market. Generally pieces were offered at the pottery or sold door to door by horse drawn wagon.

Figure 91   Early twentieth century stoneware, Whitetlall, Illinois and Ruckel's Pottery

Few potteries limited themselves in their products and most sold a full spectrum of stoneware items. These included open pots, covered pots, pans, bowls, cups, flowerpots, churns, mugs, jugs, pitchers, strainers or colanders, and spitoons.

Of these myriad of products only stoneware jugs were marked with any degree of consistency. It is possible that a marked pitcher or covered pot or butter crock will be found with the maker's impressed mark but it is not probable.

In addition to producing similar goods, the potters also typically were poor businessmen, great potters, terrible insurance risks due to kiln explosions and the constant danger of fire, and sure to go bankrupt if they stayed in business for any length of time.

They were also destined to lose a portion of their business with each new innovation that found its way into the American kitchen. In the early 1840's glass began to be massed produced and the market for stoneware mugs and bottles was greatly diminished. With the development of glass canning jars and ice boxes in the 1870's the food storage aspect of pottery was destroyed. The final blow to the few potteries that survived into the twentieth century was the advent of national Prohibition in 1919 which wiped out production for the beer, wine and liquor industries.

The value of a piece of stoneware is largely determined by the decoration it carries. Obvious exceptions to this are pieces by Commeraw, Crolius, or other rare and early makers.

There were five major techniques for decorating stoneware pottery during the nineteenth century. It is possible to gain additional insight into the age of a piece by noting how it was decorated.

Figure 92   Two gallon jug, brush painted bird, New York Stoneware Co., Fort Edward, New York, c. 1870-75

Early potters took a sharp tool or stick and scratched incised designs of fish, flowers or birds into the wet clay of the freshly formed piece. Stoneware was incised from the late 1700's until about 1830. At approximately that point various cobalt mixtures were brushed onto the surface of the pot or jug. These decorations took the forms of animals, flowers, birds, or elaborate swirls. Brush painting with cobalt slip continued until the early 1870's.

In the late 1840's and early 1850's the use of a slip cup became popular in decorating stoneware. A slip cup was used in much the same manner as a baker uses a tool to decorate cakes or cookies. The slip cup left a thick trail of cobalt slip on the surface of the pottery that can still be felt when a hand is rubbed across the decoration.

By 1870 the competition among potteries was such that it was almost impossible to pay employees to hand decorate each piece and maintain any profit margin. After this point most of the stoneware that was decorated was done with a stencil and a splash of cobalt. The stencil was placed on the pottery and brushed over.

In the 1880's and 1890's several potteries used small stamped or impressed decorations near the neck of the jugs in much the same fashion that the maker's name had been impressed since the late 1700's.

Elaborate brush decorated stoneware from the midwest is almost unknown. This is due to the late date at which most midwestern potteries were established. Cobalt swirls, numbers or simple flowers are about as involved as midwestern stoneware was decorated.

Figure 93   Two gallon, stoneware jar, deep cobalt flower, Lyons, New York, c. 1870-75

Figure 94

Figure 94 Stoneware jugs, New England, nineteenth century.

These three pieces of stoneware are representatives of the potter's craft during the nineteenth century. The pear shaped or "ovoid" three gallon jug was made prior to 1840. The "3" was stretched or incised into the neck of the jug and then brushed with cobalt slip.

The J. and E. Norton "bird" jug was made in Bennington, Vermont at some point between 1850 and 1859. The cobalt bird on the branch is unusually detailed. Compare the sides of this jug with the examples on either side. Notice the gradual progression of the jugs to the almost cylindrical form at right.

The "Shaker Brand Ketchup" jug dates from the early 1900's. It was molded rather than hand thrown and is unique only because of the stenciled Shaker label.

Figure 95 S. Risley, Norwich, Connecticut, ovoid jug, c. 1840.

Sidney Risley was in business in Norwich from the early 1840's until 1881. It is uncommon to find such elaborate brush painting on an ovoid jug.

Figure 95

Figure 96 Stoneware jugs, Bennington, Vermont, c. late 1870's.
This illustrates the form that stoneware pottery was taking in the late 1870's.

Figure 97 C.W. Braun, Buffalo, N.Y., jar, unsigned six gallon bird crock, c. 1860-1865

These two pieces of stoneware were decorated with a slip cup. The slip cup left a raised trail of cobalt slip that allowed the decorater to add unusual detail to the birds. Note the "spots" of cobalt left by the slip cup on the bodies of the two birds. Slip cupping or quill-trailing was not carried on for a lengthy period because of the time and costs incurred in the process. Brush decoration and stenciling were much more quickly completed and considerably less expensive.

Figure 98 Reproduction bird jug, c. 1978 and four gallon bird crock from Ft. Edward, New York, c. 1870.

The slip cup decorated "bird on a branch" jug dates from early 1978. The potter who made it for us incises his initials and the date on the bottom of each of his products He was forced to date his work because much of it was being sold as early pottery in a number of "antiques" shops. The first piece we saw was purchased by a dealer in Ohio for his personal collection for $125. He found it in a poorly lighted shop and surrendered to his emotions rather than to his intellect and quickly bought it.

The four gallon crock was made at the Ottman Brothers Pottery and is brush decorated. With these two pieces it is possible to compare the slip-cupping process with the more common brush painting

Figure 99

Figure 99 Six gallon brush decorated crock, F.B. Norton, Worcester, Massachusetts, c. 1860's.
Two gallon brush decorated crock, John Burger, Rochester, New York, c. 1860's.

It is a rare occurence to find a heavily decorated six gallon crock. Norton used this "parrot" on both jugs and crocks. Compare the cobalt flower on the Burger crock with the flower on the stoneware jar in Figure 93. It appears that the same decorator moved from Rochester to Lyons and took his flower with him.

Figure 100 Unsigned 1½ gallon pickling jar, c. mid-nineteenth century.
Vegetables were stored in vinegar in stone canning or pickling jars prior to the coming of glass canning jars and refrigeration in the late nineteenth century.

Figure 100

Figure 101

Figure 102

Figure 101 Brush decorated bird crock, Noah White, Utica, New York, c. 1870's.

Figure 102 Four gallon mineral spring water jug, J. Norton and Company, 1½ gallon jar from Bennington made between 1859 and 1861, and a N.A. White two gallon crock with slip cup and brush flower.

The cobalt slip was made by melting potash, silica sand, and cobalt oxide. The mixture was then ground and added to a combination of white clay and water (slip) to provide color.

Figure 103 Charles Hart, Ogdensburg, New York, four gallon crock, c. 1850-1859.   ▶

This unusual duck was caught in the process of fluttering to earth or taking off. Charles Hart was in business in Sherburne, New York from 1841 to 1850 and in Ogdensburg from 1850 to 1859. He later returned to Sherburne. Potters were basically transcients who moved from community to community as markets changed, bankruptcies occurred, or potteries were leveled by fire.

Figure 103

Figure 104

Figure 105

Figure 104 Vender's jug, canning jar, brush decorated crock from F.B. Norton, Worcester, Massachusetts, and an open jar.

Almost all eastern potteries produced jugs and crocks for specific shops or venders with the business name written on it in cobalt script. The majority of these date from the late nineteenth or early twentieth century and are still often reasonably priced.

Figure 105 Two gallon crock, Lyons, New York, c. 1860's.

Figure 106 Covered crocks, spitoons, White's Utica pitcher, nineteenth century.

The covered crocks were used to hold butter or fruit cakes. Brandy was often poured over the cake and allowed to mellow in the crock. Brush decorated spitoons are uncommon as most were broken while in service. This unsigned example dates from the first half of the nineteenth century.

Figure 107 Redware milk pans, pie plates, apple butter pots, nineteenth century

The production of redware by country potters preceeded the age of stoneware by almost a century. There were abundant deposits of red clay along the New England coast and in Pennsylvania. Redware was fired at relatively low temperatures in simple country kilns. A major problem with early redware was that it was not water tight and slowly "bled" its contents unless it was sealed or glazed. The glaze most often used was made of finely ground clay, water, and powdered red lead. The lead had a tendency to interact with the foods and liquids served or stored in the redware and a lethal poison was created. The longer the contents were left in the redware the more severe the consequences were for anyone who ate Grandma Edna's special pickles.

The apple butter pot (at left) was covered with a green glaze that was obtained from scrapings of copper oxide.

Figure 106

Figure 107

Figure 108 Redware cottage cheese mold, two pots, and a pie plate, Pennsylvania, first half of the nineteenth century.

Figure 109 Sleepy Eye Flour premiums, produced by the Monmouth Pottery, Monmouth, Illinois, early twentieth century.

Baskets

The decade of the 1970's saw a discovery of the art of the basketmaker and his wares by the mass of collectors of country antiques. Baskets that did not sell when offered for $35 in 1970 could not be found to buy for $135 in 1980. In almost any magazine today dealing with colonial or country furnishings, baskets are a critical aspect of the decorating design.

Baskets produced by country craftsmen were designed for utility and not for decoration. Basketmakers used oak and ash splints, vines, twigs, and rye straw to make a multitude of basket forms with almost all designated for a specific purpose or job.

For example, hexagon woven open cheese or curd baskets were made to be placed over a stoneware crock and serve as a sieve when a mixture of curds and whey was poured through the cheese cloth placed in the basket. The whey passed through the cloth and the curds remained. The curds were folded in the cloth and allowed to dry. The whey was then poured from the crock into buckets for the pigs to feast upon.

Baskets were built for use in the fields, the orchard, the berry patch, the flower and herb garden, and for carrying home the bacon from the store. General purpose or utility baskets were also constructed in large quantities throughout the nineteenth century. Unfortunately, relatively few of these early baskets have survived because of the constant exposure to water, dirt, mud, careless hands, over loading, and the little regard in which they were held by their owners.

When the bottom fell out or the handle was split the basket was discarded. They were plentiful, inexpensive, and in constant use. They were purchased or bartered from traveling families of basket makers and in small towns that housed a population of basketmakers. The basketmakers charged little for their wares because nature provided the raw materials and a sharp knife was relatively inexpensive.

The era of basketmaking by craftsmen was largely destroyed by 1900 with the introduction of machines that cut and prepared the splint in wide and thick bands and turned out galvanized handles and metal staples to bind the basket together. By 1900 square willow clothes hampers were priced at $3 and round hampers for $2.30. Lunch baskets, willow and splint clothes baskets, and market baskets of rattan, splint, or white bleached willow were also offered.

The simple country baskets that unconsciously followed the Shaker philosophy of form following function no longer were marketable in an era in love with color and style. A lunch basket that sold for $1.25 was advertised as made of "braided straw and fancy colored willows, hinged top with latch; very fancy."

Country baskets continued to be made on a limited basis in isolated outposts of craftsmenship in Appalachia and New England but even these areas eventually gave in to the inexpensive and massed produced baskets that became available as roads and transportation improved in the twentieth century.

Figure 110 Wall of early basket forms

Figure 111 Field basket, rib construction, New England, mid-nineteenth century. 32" x 16" high.

Figure 112 Exceptionally large field basket, over 8' in circumference, made of approximately 650' to 700' of prepared ash splint, 33" diameter, 24" high, strong handles 6" wide x 1" across, possibly Shaker, New England, mid to late nineteenth century.

Figure 113 Field or orchard basket, oak splint, carved handles, rib construction, late nineteenth century, 30" diameter.

Figure 114 Field basket, rib construction, great wrapped handle, late nineteenth century, oak splint, 31" x 18" x 13" to the top of the handle.

Figure 111

Figure 112

Figure 113

Figure 114

Figure 115 Storage or gathering basket, ash with double wrapped hickory handle, rib construction, late nineteenth century, found in New England.

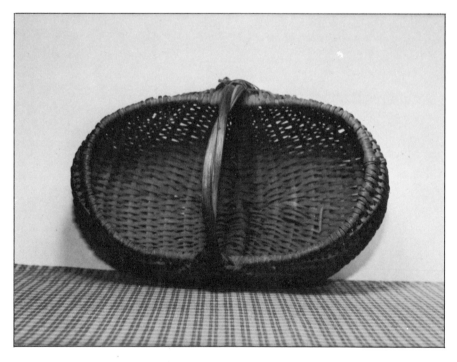

Figure 116 Interior of the gathering basket

This is a modification of the buttocks form that distributed the weight of the basket's contents to both sides rather than concentrating it in the middle of the basket.

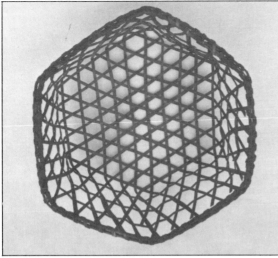

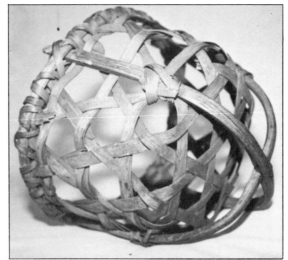

Figure 117   Figure 118

Figure 117 Drying basket for herbs, hexagon woven, six sided rim, mid to late nineteenth century, New England.

The hexagon or "cheese" weave is found in curd baskets, drying baskets, and egg baskets.

Figure 118 Ox muzzle, New England, late eighteenth or early nineteenth century, oak splint, 10" long, diameter of 12", hand forged iron nails.

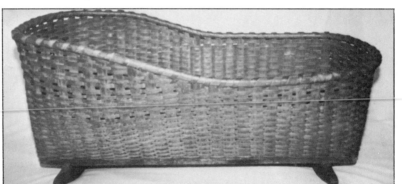

Figure 119

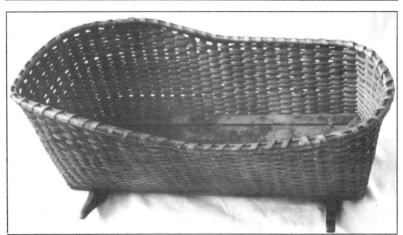

Figure 120

Figure 119 Ash splint cradle, pine base and rockers, hand forged iron nails, traces of red stain, early nineteenth century 41" long x 16" high, New England.

Figure 120 (second picture of the cradle)

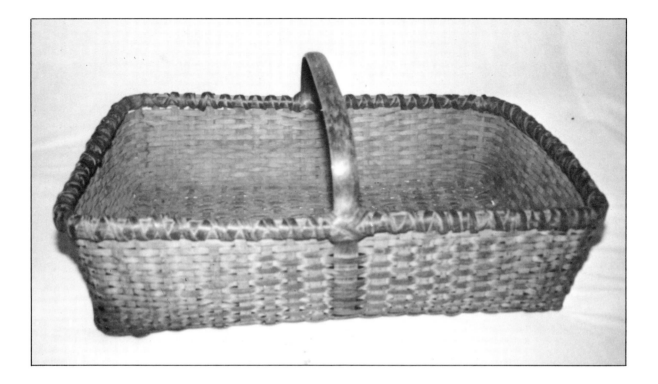

Figure 121 Splint basket, 30" long x 20" wide x 12" high to handle.

The collector who bought this basket in Indiana in 1975 indicates he was told it had originally been found in Tennessee where it was purchased from an elderly lady who called it a "pillow" basket. A pillow was placed in the basket, a baby was nestled on the pillow, and the basket, pillow, and baby were carried away. The basket appears at first look to be a more conventional gathering basket for flowers or herbs but there is a minimum amount of wear on the interior. The handle has an exceptional patina which suggests it was used a great deal.

It is difficult often times to determine specifically what function a basket served. Curd baskets and ox muzzles are obvious exceptions to this statement. It is very possible that this example was a "pillow" basket. The provenance, or alledged history of the basket, is believable and the form of the basket would lend itself to that use. Many baskets were constructed for a specific purpose for a particular individual or family. When the basket passes on to another owner, its original function is often lost to the idle speculation of a series of eventual owners.

Figure 122 Wall basket, mid-nineteenth century, New England, poplar splint, 12'' x 9'' x 6'' high.

Figure 123 Half basket, hickory handle, ash splint, late nineteenth - early twentieth century.

Figure 124   (second picture of the half basket)

Figure 125 Shaker "fancy" basket, New England, 6½" long x 3½" wide, New England, c. 1880-1910.

This basket was sold in one of the "sisters' shops" in a New England Shaker community around the turn of the century. The sisters made baskets to sell to visitors and tourists well into the twentieth century.

Figure 126 Market basket, probably Shaker, copper rivets, New England, early twentieth century.

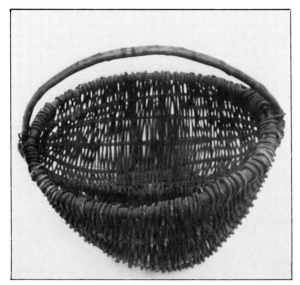

Figure 127 Gathering basket, midwestern, early twentieth century, made from wild grape vines.

Figure 128 Utility basket, ash splint, rib construction, carved oak handles, late nineteenth century, 20" high x 18" diameter.

Figure 129 Rare three handled basket, poplar splint, 13" high x 14" wide

Figure 130 Utility basket, unusually thick carved oak handle, demijohn bottom, oak splint, found in southern Illinois, c. 1900.

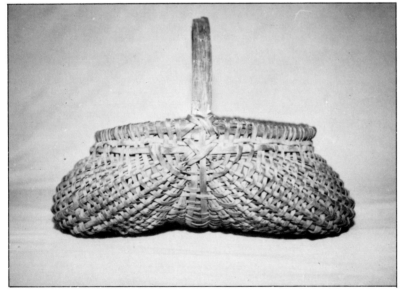

Figure 131 Gizzard or modified buttocks basket, ash splint, found in Tennessee, 10½" high to handles x 16" across.

The specific purpose of a basket like this cannot be determined. It was obviously designed to be used to carry fairly heavy fruits or vegetables because the thick, center piece of splint serves to force the contents to either side of the basket.

Figure 132 Gathering basket, New England, ash splint, mid to late nineteenth century, 8"
high to handle, 6" wide x 9" long.

Stains on the inside of the basket indicate it may have been used on berry picking excursions.

Figure 133 Oval field basket, low feet carved from the runners that reinforce the bottom,
oak splint, mid to late nineteenth century, 28" x 17" x 11" high to handles.

Footed baskets are not often found. The addition of feet to a basket generally indicates that
it was also used to dry the contents by allowing air to easily pass under the basket and circulate throughout it.

Figure 134

Figure 135

Figure 134 Rye straw utility basket, Pennsylvania, hickory handle, mid-nineteenth century.

Figure 135 Handle of the coil construction rye straw basket

Figure 136

Figure 137

Figure 136 Swing handle basket, rib construction, demijohn or "kicked-up" bottom, New England, nineteenth century.

Figure 137 Swing handle basket, rib construciton, demijohn bottom, New England, nineteenth century.

The "kicked-up" bottom distributed the basket's contents evenly in the interior of the basket.

Figure 138 Demijohn or "kicked-up" bottom

Figure 139 Rectangular swing handle
basket, oak splint, found in Vermont,
nineteenth century

Figure 140 Bottom of swing handle
basket.

The carved oak runners on the bottom of a basket added to its strength and its ability to
hold up under heavy use.

Figure 141 Pinned swing handle

Figure 142 Swing handle

Figure 143   Pine reinforced bottom of swing handle basket

Figure 144

Figure 144 Plaited or checker worked bottom

The simplest form of making a bottom for a basket that is not designed for carrying heavy loads, is plaiting or checker working. It is a pattern of one under and one over repeatedly.

Figure 145 "Cheese-weave" baskets, New England, Mid-nineteenth century.

The handled drying basket (at left) was constructed with the same hexagon weave as the two curd or cheese baskets. In the mid-1970's, a cheese basket could be purchased for $150 with a moderate amount of inconvenience. By early 1980 a standard price for the baskets was $300 with a significant amount of inconvenience involved. They have reached the point when badly damaged baskets are being skillfully repaired and fakes are appearing in the market place. The new baskets are "fakes" and not reproductions. A reproduction is made to provide an alternative for someone who does not have the desire or money to purchase the earlier version. The seller and buyer each understands the situation when the sale is consummated. A "fake" is what the term implies. The seller is usually aware of his merchandise and the buyer is not. The purpose of the "fake" is to deceive.

Figure 146 Windsor cheese drainer, New England, first half of the nineteenth century.

In using a woven cheese basket, it was necessary to have a "ladder" to put over the crock with the basket and cheese cloth placed on the "ladder". The mixture of curds and whey was then poured through the cloth. This drainer has a ladder attached.

Figure 147 Painted baskets, New England, nineteenth century

Figure 148 Nantucket Lightship basket, rib construction, rattan, wooden bottom, swing handle, Nantucket, Massachusetts, c. 1900.

The primary characteristic of Nantucket baskets that differentiates them from most baskets is that they are woven of rattan rather than oak or ash splint. The rattan was brought to Nantucket from the Phillipines, China, or India by sailors returning from long trade or whaling voyages. The baskets also have distinctive turned wooden bottoms and were made on molds.

Figure 149

Figure 150

Figure 149 Field basket, late nineteenth century, oak splint, carved oak handles, 30'' diameter.

This basket was used to carry root crops or garden vegetables from the field. The open weave of the bottom allowed the accumulated dirt to fall through and the contents to be scrubbed down before being carted into the kitchen.

Figure 150 Field basket, ash and hickory splint, midwestern, late nineteenth-early twentieth century, found in central Illinois, 29'' diameter.

Figure 151 Uncommonly large field basket, Maine, mid-nineteenth century, ash splint, 41'' x 26'' x 11'' deep

Figure 152   Herb gathering basket, found in Conn., late nineteenth century, carved handles.

Figure 153 Collection of utility baskets in a variety of forms.

Figure 154 Variety of ash and oak splint baskets

In the center of these baskets is a classic example of a factory-made basket from some point in the twentieth century. It is impossible to date because production techniques varied little from the 1880's until the mid-1900's. The standard size of the machine cut splint and handle may be contrasted with the wide variety of techniques utilized in the hand crafted baskets in the same picture.

Each piece of splint in the factory-made basket is precisely the same because it was cut from a veneering machine that was disgustingly consistent. There are no tool marks on the handle because it too was created by machine. These baskets were cheaply made and sold to hardware or grocery stores and apple and produce growers.

Figure 155 Feather basket, early to mid-nineteenth century, Maine, ash splint, 26" high x 20" at the widest point

Figure 156 Willow garden basket, early twentieth century

Odds and Ends

This particular chapter was the easiest to put together because the items included obviously fit no where else in the book. We have provided illustrations of a wide variety of kitchen and hearth related antiques (some are not close relations but are still in the family) that are of special interest to us.

Think of this chapter much like the "People" section of *Time*. The individuals and events are certainly not significant but they are interesting and well worth your time.

The items range from restaurant signs (*kitchen* related) to samplers (working in front of the *hearth* on cold winter evenings related) to valentines (something to give to mother for working in the *kitchen* so hard related).

Figure 157 Wall coffee grinders, c. 1910

Figure 158 Cast iron apple peeler, c. 1900

Figure 159 Home pencil sharpener, c. 1920

Figure 160 Iron cherry pitter, c. 1920

Figure 161 Cream can, Fedder Dairy, Collinsville, Illinois, c. 1925

Figure 162 Handcrafted bed key for tightening rope beds, c. 1840

Figure 163 Tin cookie cutter, late nineteenth century

Figure 164 Advertising bag for baking powder, early twentieth century

Figure 165 Washing powder box, c. 1910

Figure 166 Punched paper "practice" sampler, Pennsylvania, dated 1854

Figure 167 Restaurant sign, pine, New England, late nineteenth century.

In decorating a house, a corner, or a kitchen with country antiques it is essential that the attitude and atmosphere be relaxed. The "Farmer's Lunch Room and Bakery" unquestionably had great breakfasts and spectacular doughnuts. It is not hard to visualize walking into the lunch room on a Saturday morning at seven o'clock with the smell of bacon, coffee, and fresh bakery goods cutting the air and mingling with the talk of farmers, shop keepers, and fishermen.

To compare the ways our lives have been altered, mentally paint your own picture of the "Farmer's Lunch Room and Bakery". Include the building, the counter, tables and chairs, the conversations and the customers.

Now erase the images you have just conjured up and paint a picture of breakfast at the McDonald's on the next block or in a neighboring town.

Figure 167

Figure 168

Figure 169

Figure 168 ''City Candy Kitchen Restaurant'' sign, tin framed with pine, c. 1930.

What is a plain dope?

Figure 169 Collection of Shaker seed boxes, Mt. Lebanon, New York, c. 1858-1890.

The Mt. Lebanon Shakers were the first to sell seeds in individual packets. Prior to the Shakers entering the seed industry, seeds were sold only in bulk. The Shakers distributed the boxes and seeds to urban and rural stores on a consignment basis. The Shakers returned each fall to pick up their money, excess seeds, and the boxes.

Figure 170 Hiram Sibley seed packets or "papers", c. 1890.

We have some friends who have collected country store antiques for many years and recreated their own store. They have searched in vain for several years for a Hiram Sibley seed box. It was too much to hope to find any packets of late nineteenth century Sibley garden seeds.

We were in Lancaster County, Pennsylvania several years ago and stopped in a roadside shop. As we searched through the pottery, baskets, and related pieces of furniture, my wife spotted a seed box with the exterior label intact. In fact, it was a Hiram Sibley seed box complete with a full compliment of seed bundles and packets. Did we sell the box and seeds to our friends? No, but we gave them a packet and began a seed box collection of our own.

Figure 171 Collection of seed boxes, tins, and painted boxes in a country kitchen.

Figure 172 Iron toaster and brass skimmer from Pennsylvania, c. 1840.

Figure 173 Collection of copper jelly or pudding molds, late nineteenth century.

There are a wide variety of food molds in tin, pewter, wood, copper, stoneware, china, or glass. Puddings, jellies, butter, ice cream, cakes, gingerbread, maple sugar, and cookies were commonly produced or shaped in molds that added a visual touch to meals and pride for the cook or baker.

Figure 174 Valentines or inexpensive gifts made in Europe for Pennsylvania Germans in the mid-nineteenth century.

The two pictures at right carry the messages "Forget Me Not" and "Out of Love."

Figure 175 Stack of home-
spun material, nineteenth
century.

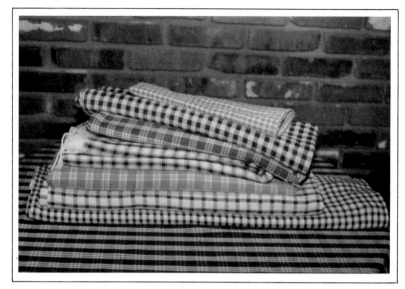

Included in this stack are
two homespun bed-ticks. The
bed-tick served as a mattress.
It was filled with straw and
placed on top of the ropes that
crisscrossed the frame and
held the bed together. On top
of the straw filled bed-tick was
often a large pillow filled with
feathers in the winter or corn
husks in the summer that provided additional comfort.
The piece of dark blue and white "homespun" on which the stack rests is a reproduction
that is made by Eagerty for Cohasset Colonial.

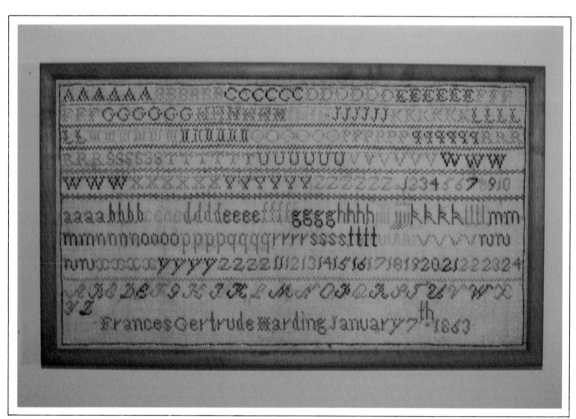

Figure 176 Sampler of Francis Gertrude Harding, dated January 7, 1863

Figure 177 Sampler of Jennette Elizabeth Fitch, aged 10 years, undated.

Figure 178 Shaker Pickles, E.D. Pettengill, Portland, Maine, c. 1900. Shaker Horse Radish, E.D. Pettengill, Portland, Maine, c. 1900.

Figure 179 Collection of cream and milk bottles, twentieth century.

An area that has not been explored by many collectors today is the finding of milk and cream bottles from early twentieth century dairies. The dairy in our town gave up the use of glass bottles in December, 1979 and has turned to plastic. The dairy has not really turned to plastic but the world has.

The spoon was used to skim cream off the top of the opened bottle of milk. It dates from the 1920's and was probably a premium or given away by the local diary.

Figure 180 Child's sewing machine, iron and trivet, collection of sad irons, late nineteenth century-early twentieth century.

The term "sad iron" refers to an iron that is solid or heavy. It may be contrasted with a "box" iron that is hollow and has a door at the back of the iron for a small heated brick to be slipped inside.

Figure 181 Fluting machines, crimping iron, goffering or finishing iron, and wood framed tin foot warmer.

The history of the household iron goes as far back as recorded history. The Vikings used hot stones and Koreans used pieces of heated brass with wooden or bone handles.

The crimping iron was used for gathering and pleating ruffles and dates from about 1870. The goffering or fin-

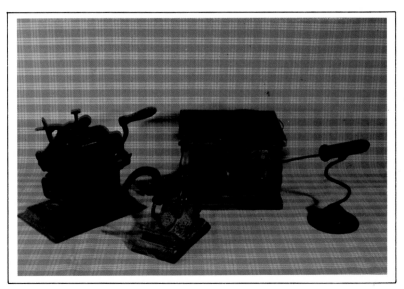

ishing iron was removed from its holder and was heated in the fireplace. It was then placed back in the holder and coat sleeves, shirt collars, trousers, or shirt cuffs were moved up and down against the holder to remove wrinkles. The goffering iron dates from the early 1800's.

The foot warmer dates from about 1850 and contains a small pan that was filled with hot coals from the fireplace and placed in the pierced tin warmer. Foot warmers were used in the home, for long sermons on cold Sunday mornings, and in sleighs to combat the winter winds on the ride home.

Figure 182 Ice sign, soap saver, ice cream scoop, chopping knife, pot scrubber, tin funnel, factory-made kitchen ware from the early twentieth century.

The ice sign could be a rarity because it's the only one we have ever seen. However, we have no conscious memory of ever purposefully looking for an ice sign. The homemaker who needed ice in 1915 for her oak ice box put the sign in the window to communicate to the iceman exactly how much was necessary. Based on this photograph, we have just ordered a fifty pound block of ice.

Figure 183 Granite ware lunch box, measure, Royal Granite Steelware miniature pans, and a funnel, early twentieth century.

Index

Index

Complimentary Value Guide to

The Collector's Guide to KITCHEN ANTIQUES

By

DON & CAROL RAYCRAFT

There is significant geographical influence on the value of country antiques. What may be eagerly collected in Maine or New York may be almost unknown outside the small group of hardcore collectors in Iowa and Utah. The recent influx of a wide variety of magazines specializing in capturing the elusive "country" look in the American home will provide a foundation of information for readers across the nation and probably raise prices as even more collectors enter the tighty crowded market place.

In attempting to ascertain value of the items pictured in our book, we have provided a wide price range. This is necessitated by the constantly changing market.

The Country Home

Lighting

Woodenware

Fig. 82 Chopping bowl — $100.00-$125.00
rolling pins, butter molds
Fig. 83 Piggin — $55.00-$75.00
Fig. 84 Maple sugar mold — $90.00-$120.00; pastry print
— $100.00-$120.00
Fig. 85 Stack of Shaker boxes — $250.00-$450.00
(depending on size)
Fig. 86 Shaker boxes — $250.00-$350.00
Fig. 87 Large Shaker box — $500.00-$550.00
Fig. 88 Carriers — $450.00-$550.00
Fig. 89 Pantry boxes — $45.00-$60.00
Fig. 90 Serving tray — $200.00-$275.00

Pottery
Fig. 91 White Hall and Ruckel pottery — $35.00-$200.00
Fig. 92 Fort Edward "bird" jug — $225.00-$300.00
Fig. 93 Lyons stoneware jar — $175.00-$225.00
Fig. 94 New England stoneware jugs — $275.00-$350.00;
$250.00-300.00; $175.00-$200.00
Fig. 95 Risley ovoid jug — $275.00-$325.00
Fig. 96 Stoneware jugs — $150.00-$200.00
Fig. 97 Braun jar — $300.00-$350.00; unsigned "bird"
crock — $300.00-375.00
Fig. 98 Reproduction jug ; "bird" crock —
$250.00-$275.00
Fig. 99 Norton "bird" crock — $350.00-$400.00;
Burger crock — $200.00-$250.00
Fig. 100 Pickling jar — $150.00-$175.00
Fig. 101 White "bird" crock — $250.00-$275.00
Fig. 102 Mineral Spring jug — $250.00-$275.00; Benn-
ington "bird" jar — $200.00-$250.00; White crock
— $150.00-$175.00
Fig. 103 Hart "bird" crock — $325.00-$375.00
Fig. 104 Vender's jug — $70.00-$80.00; canning jar —
$55.00-$65.00; brush decorated crock —
$135.00-$150.00; and an open jar — $25.00-$30.00
Fig. 105 Lyons crock — $150.00-$175.00
Fig. 106 Covered crocks — $275.00-$375.00; spittoons —
$220.00-$250.00; pitcher — $100.00-$125.00
Fig. 107 Redware milk pans, pie plates, apple butter pots
— $75.00-$150.00
Fig. 108 Cheese mold, pots, and a pie plate —
$75.00-$100.00
Fig. 109 Sleepy Eye premiums — $150.00-$200.00 (each)

Baskets
Fig. 111 Field basket — $250.00-$325.00
Fig. 112 Large field basket — $225.00-$275.00
Fig. 113 Field basket — $175.00-$200.00
Fig. 114 Field basket - $250.00-$300.00
Fig. 115 Storage or gathering basket — $300.00-$350.00
Fig. 117 Drying basket — $250.00-$275.00
Fig. 118 Ox muzzle — $150.00-$175.00
Fig. 119 Spling cradle — $700.00-$850.00
Fig. 121 "Pillow" basket — $175.00-$225.00
Fig. 122 Wall basket — $70.00-$85.00
Fig. 123 Half basket — $150.00-$185.00
Fig. 125 Shaker "fancy" basket — $125.00-$150.00
Fig. 126 Market basket — $150.00-$170.00
Fig. 127 Gathering basket — $50.00-$70.00
Fig. 128 Three-handled basket — $75.00-$90.00
Fig. 129 Utility basket — $75.00-$85.00
Fig. 130 Utility basket — $65.00-$75.00
Fig. 131 Gizzard basket — $75.00-$125.00
Fig. 132 Gathering basket — $80.00-$90.00
Fig. 133 Oval field basket — $125.00-$140.00

Fig. 134 Rye straw utility basket — $135.00-$150.00
Fig. 136 Swing handle basket — $200.00-$250.00
Fig. 137 Swing handle basket — $200.00-$250.00
Fig. 139 Rectangular swing handle basket —
$225.00-$275.00
Fig. 145 "Cheese" weave baskets — $225.00-$400.00
Fig. 146 Windsor cheese drainer — $325.00-$425.00
Fig. 147 Painted baskets — $200.00-$400.00
Fig. 148 Nantucket lightship basket — $350.00-$450.00
Fig. 149 Field basket — $200.00-$225.00
Fig. 150 Field basket — $300.00-$350.00
Fig. 151 Uncommonly large field basket —
$300.00-$350.00
Fig. 152 Herb gathering basket — $150.00-$175.00
Fig. 153 Collection of utility baskets — $70.00-$95.00
Fig. 154 Classic factory-made basket — $25.00-$35.00
Fig. 155 Feather basket — $250.00-$300.00
Fig. 156 Willow garden basket — $35.00-$45.00

Odds & Ends
Fig. 157 Wall coffee grinder — $65.00-$75.00
Fig. 158 Apple peeler — $60.00-$70.00
Fig. 159 Pencil sharpener — $25.00-$35.00
Fig. 160 Cherry pitter — $30.00-$35.00
Fig. 161 Cream can — $70.00-$85.00
Fig. 162 Bed key — $25.00-$30.00
Fig. 163 Cookie cutter — $50.00-$75.00
Fig. 164 Advertising bag — $12.00-$16.00
Fig. 165 Washing powder box — $20.00-$24.00
Fig. 166 "Practice" sampler — $95.00-$120.00
Fig. 167 Restaurant Sign — $375.00-$425.00
Fig. 168 Restaurant Sign — $200.00-$275.00
Fig. 169 Shaker seed boxes — $250.00-$550.00
Fig. 170 Seed packets — $6.00-$8.00 (each)
Fig. 171 Seed boxes and painted boxes —
$100.00-$300.00
Fig. 172 Toaster — $150.00-$175.00; skimmer —
$100.00-$125.00
Fig. 173 Copper molds — $50.00-$70.00 (each)
Fig. 174 Valentines — $50.00-$60.00 (each)
Fig. 175 Stack of homespun — $70.00-$300.00
Fig. 176 Sampler — $225.00-$250.00
Fig. 177 Sampler — $125.00-$160.00
Fig. 178 Shaker bottles — $175.00-$200.00;
$100.00-$125.00
Fig. 179 Milk bottles — $8.00-$10.00 (each)
Fig. 180 Child's sewing machine — $120.00-$140.00
Fig. 181 Fluting machines — $50.00-$150.00
Fig. 182 Ice sign — $20.00-$30.00; soap saver —
$8.00-$10.00; scoop — $6.00-$8.00; chopping
knife — $12.00-$14.00
Fig. 183 Graniteware lunch box — $20.00-$24.00; measure
— $6.00-$9.00; miniature pans — $8.00-$10.00
(each); and funnel — $14.00-$16.00

cb COLLECTOR BOOKS

Box 3009   Paducah, Kentucky 42001